The Ethical E~~dge~~

Handling Tech Trends and AI Bias Issues

Taylor Royce

DEDICATION

To the trailblazers and visionaries who work to use technology to advance society. This book is dedicated to individuals who are dedicated to negotiating the difficulties of contemporary advancements with integrity and accountability, and who think that ethics and innovation may coexist.

May this work serve as an inspiration for a time when technology will empower and uplift all people, guiding progress along the lines of justice, openness, and respect for each and every one of them.

To my friends and family, without whose steadfast encouragement and support this journey would not have been possible. I appreciate your faith in me and the possibility of a more morally upright future.

And to all of the readers, thinkers, and doers who work to comprehend and mold the ethical edge of technology may we all work together to create a future in which human values and technological achievements coexist together

CONTENTS

ACKNOWLEDGMENTS

I want to express my sincere gratitude to everyone who helped make this book possible.

Above all, I owe a debt of gratitude to my family for their constant support and inspiration along this trip. Your patience and faith in my vision have been my sources of inspiration and strength.

The content of this book has been greatly influenced by the ideas and skills of my colleagues and mentors in the realms of ethics and technology. Your commitment to increasing understanding and encouraging moral behavior in the field of technology has been an inspiration.

A special thank you to all of the experts and thinking leaders who so kindly gave of their time and insights. Your contributions have improved this study and given us a better grasp of the intricate problems relating to technology and artificial intelligence.

Thank you to my editors and the publishing crew for their

painstaking attention to detail and dedication to quality, which have made this book match the highest standards. Your advice has been very helpful in making this endeavor a success.

In addition, I would like to thank all of the numerous academics, professionals, and activists whose contributions to the fields of AI ethics, data privacy, and human rights have influenced and enlightened the conversations in this book. Your commitment to building a just and equitable digital environment is admirable and crucial.

Lastly, I would like to say to all of the readers who interact with this book that the quest for a better future is fueled by your interest and dedication to comprehending the ethical implications of technology. This book is presented with the hopes of igniting important discussion and action.

We appreciate your support, donations, and conviction about the significance of ethical technology, everyone.

Disclaimer

The Ethical Edge: Handling Tech Trends and AI Bias Issues contains information that is solely meant to be instructive and informative. The author's views and opinions are the only ones that are represented in this book and do not necessarily represent the official policies or positions of any associated companies, institutions, or organizations.

Even though every attempt has been taken to guarantee the precision and entirety of the data presented in this book, certain facts may become old due to the quick evolution of technology. It is recommended that readers confirm any technical, legal, or policy information with current sources and get guidance from appropriate professionals on particular matters.

Any mistakes, omissions, or results from using or interpreting the information in this book are not the responsibility of the author or publisher. The reader takes full responsibility for any decisions they take based on the information in this book, and the material presented here is not intended to replace professional consultation or guidance.

You recognize and agree to this disclaimer by reading this book.

CHAPTER 1

Artificial Intelligence (AI): Transforming Our World

1.1 AI: A Comprehensive Overview of Its Nature and Functions

Although artificial intelligence (AI) has gained popularity in contemporary technology and media, comprehending its fundamental ideas is necessary to fully appreciate its significance and promise. Artificial Intelligence (AI) is the emulation of human intelligence in machines that are intended to behave and think like people. These artificial intelligence systems possess the ability to learn from their experiences, adjust to novel inputs, and carry out activities that conventionally demand for human intelligence.

Primary AI Components:

Data: Data forms the basis of AI. Large volumes of data are processed, analyzed, and interpreted by machines to identify trends and make judgments.

- **Methods:** These are the equations and principles of mathematics that let computers learn from data. Simple linear regressions and intricate neural networks are two examples of algorithms.

- **Machine Learning (ML):** A branch of artificial intelligence, ML is concerned with creating algorithms that let computers analyze, interpret, and learn from data. As ML models are exposed to additional data, they get better over time.

- **In-Depth Education:** 'Deep' learning, another kind of machine learning, uses many-layered neural networks. These networks are the foundation of many contemporary AI systems and are capable of modeling intricate patterns in huge datasets.

1.2 The State of AI: From Deep Learning to Machine Learning

The field of artificial intelligence is broad and includes a variety of approaches and technology. Comprehending the differences and relationships among various forms of artificial intelligence is essential to recognizing its strengths and weaknesses.

1.2.1 Machine Learning (ML):

ML is a data analysis technique that uses automation to generate analytical models. It is predicated on the notion that machines are capable of learning from data, spotting patterns, and making judgments with little help from humans. Important forms of machine learning are as follows:

1. **Supervised Learning:** involves labeled dataset training, where each training example has an output label associated with it. Regression and classification tasks are common uses.

2. **Unsupervised Learning:** entails using unlabeled data to train a model. With common uses including association and clustering, the system attempts to infer structure and patterns from the data.

3. **Reinforcement Learning:** A sort of learning in which an agent picks up decision-making skills by acting in a way that maximizes the total cumulative reward in a given environment. It is extensively utilized in gaming and robotics.

1.2.2 Deep Learning:

Deep learning, a branch of machine learning, employs multi-layered neural networks (deep networks) to examine different aspects of data. Deep learning models, in contrast to conventional machine learning models, are able to autonomously extract from raw data the representations required for feature identification or classification.

- **Intelligent Systems:** These algorithms, which are composed of layers of connected nodes (neurons), are modeled after the structure of the human brain. Every link serves as a synapse, and every node functions as a synthetic neuron.

- **CNNs, or convolutional neural networks:** CNNs are primarily utilized for the automatic and adaptive learning of spatial hierarchies of information in images and videos.

- **RNNs (Recurrent Neural Networks):** RNNs may retain recollection of past inputs because of their directed cycle connections, which make them appropriate for sequential data such as time series or spoken language.

1.3 AI's Practical Uses in Transforming Industries

AI is transforming a number of industries by streamlining workflows, increasing productivity, and stimulating creativity. Some of the main areas where AI is having a big impact are listed below:

1.3.1 Healthcare:

By enhancing patient care, therapy, and diagnosis, AI is revolutionizing the medical field.

- **Diagnostics:** AI systems are more accurate than human radiologists at analyzing medical pictures (such as MRIs and X-rays) and identifying problems.

- **Personalized Medicine:** AI can evaluate patient data to forecast a patient's response to a medication, allowing for individualized treatment regimens.

- **Administrative work:** Healthcare personnel can concentrate more on patient care by delegating scheduling, billing, and other administrative work to AI-powered systems.

1.3.2 Finance:

Artificial intelligence has a lot to offer the finance sector in terms of trading, risk management, and fraud detection.

- **Fraud Detection:** By examining transaction patterns and identifying anomalous activity, AI systems can drastically cut down on fraudulent activity.

- **Algorithmic Trading:** AI-powered algorithms are able to evaluate enormous volumes of data in real time, which allows them to make investment decisions quicker and with greater accuracy than human traders.

- **Customer Service:** AI-driven chatbots and virtual assistants offer round-the-clock assistance to consumers, enhancing their pleasure and cutting down on overhead.

1.3.3 Transportation:

Autonomous vehicles, traffic control, and predictive maintenance are some of the ways artificial intelligence is advancing the transportation industry.

- **Autonomous Vehicles:** Businesses like Tesla and Waymo are using artificial intelligence (AI) to create self-driving cars that can navigate and react to traffic situations without the need for human intervention.

- **Traffic Management:** To ease congestion and enhance traffic flow, AI systems can examine traffic patterns and adjust signal timings.
- **Predictive Maintenance:** Artificial intelligence (AI) can forecast when a car or infrastructure part is likely to break, enabling prompt maintenance and cutting downtime.

1.3.4 Retail:

AI improves customer service, streamlines inventory control, and tailors marketing tactics in the retail industry.

- **consumer Experience:** AI-powered recommendation engines make product recommendations based on past browsing activity and consumer preferences.
- **Inventory Management:** AI systems are able to optimize inventory levels and forecast demand trends, which lowers costs and boosts productivity.
- **Personalized Marketing:** AI uses consumer data analysis to develop ads that are more engaging and have higher conversion rates.

1.4 The Prospects and Forecasts for AI in the Future

AI has a bright future ahead of it, with forecasts pointing to its continuous growth and permeation into many facets of our existence. Here are some significant patterns and forecasts:

1.4.1 Better AI-Human Cooperation:

AI will gradually enhance human abilities rather than take their place, resulting in more productive and successful teamwork. This kind of cooperation will be observed in industries such as healthcare, where AI can help physicians with diagnosis and treatment planning, and education, where AI can offer tailored learning opportunities.

1.4.2 General AI:

AI will permeate every aspect of our daily life as it is increasingly incorporated into commonplace goods and services. Wearable technology, digital assistants that are tailored to each user, and smart homes will all grow in sophistication and popularity.

1.4.3 AI Ethics:

As AI develops, ethical issues will become more and more important. Preventing biases and safeguarding privacy will require AI systems to have fairness, transparency, and accountability. The creation of rules and frameworks for AI ethics will be crucial in directing the ethical application of AI.

1.4.4 Self-governing Systems:

The emergence of autonomous systems, such as robots, drones, and self-driving automobiles, will alter industries and our way of living and working. These technologies will enhance productivity, security, and ease of use across a range of industries, including transportation, logistics, healthcare, and agriculture.

1.4.5 AI in Climate Action:

AI will optimize energy use, enhance resource management, and improve environmental monitoring, all of which will be important in combating climate change. AI-driven models have the ability to minimize carbon footprints across industries, maximize renewable energy sources, and forecast climatic patterns.

Artificial intelligence is changing the world by improving human capabilities, reshaping industries, and influencing the future. It is crucial to address ethical issues and make sure AI is created and used properly for the benefit of everybody as we continue to explore its potential.

CHAPTER 2

CONNECTING EVERYTHING WITH THE INTERNET OF THINGS (IoT)

2.1 Recognizing the Platforms, Networks, and Devices in the Internet of Things Ecosystem

The network of linked devices that communicate and share data with one another over the internet is known as the Internet of Things (IoT). This ecosystem is made up of many parts that cooperate to allow intelligent operations and seamless connectivity.

2.1.1 Devices:

- **Sensors:** The main data collectors in the Internet of Things are these. Sensors gather data that may be examined by measuring a wide range of characteristics, including motion, light, temperature, humidity, and more.

- **Motors:** Based on the data they receive, these devices take actions like opening a valve, turning on a light, or modifying the thermostat.

- **Smart Electronics:** These are integrated systems, such wearable health monitors, refrigerators with smart features, and thermostats that incorporate sensors, actuators, and networking to accomplish particular tasks.

2.1.2 Networks:

- **Technologies of Connectivity:** The communication network that permits data transfer between devices is the foundation of the Internet of Things. Wi-Fi, Bluetooth, Zigbee, LoRaWAN, and cellular networks (4G/5G) are examples of common technologies.

- **Cutting-Edge Computing:** Instead of sending data to a central cloud server, edge computing processes data closer to the point of generation, reducing latency and increasing efficiency. Applying this in real-time is essential.

- **Computing on the Cloud:** The cloud offers scalable computational and storage capacity, making it possible to gather, process, and analyze data from a variety of IoT devices.

2.1.3 Platforms:

- **Internet of Things Platforms:** These are software programs for handling Internet of Things devices, information, and programs. They offer features including data analytics, application development, and device administration. Amazon Web Services (AWS) IoT, Google Cloud IoT, and Microsoft Azure IoT are a few examples.

- **Analytics of Data:** In order to facilitate insights and well-informed decision-making, IoT platforms frequently come with analytics tools that aid in processing and analyzing the massive volumes of data created by IoT devices.

2.2 Smart Cities and Homes: Changing the Way People Live

The Internet of Things (IoT) is changing the way we live by making cities and homes smarter, more connected spaces that provide increased sustainability, efficiency, and convenience.

2.2.1 Smart Homes:

- **Home Automation:** The Internet of Things makes it possible to automate a number of home operations, including heating, lighting, and security. Smartphones and voice assistants like Google Assistant and Amazon Alexa can be used to remotely operate smart home installations.

- **Management of Energy:** Energy monitors and smart thermostats maximize energy use, cutting expenses and their negative effects on the environment. They pick up on user preferences and modify settings to maximize efficiency and comfort.

- **Security Systems:** Smart locks, cameras, and motion sensors are examples of IoT-powered security systems that improve home security with real-time monitoring and warnings.

2.2.2 Smart Cities:

- **Traffic Management:** Real-time traffic condition monitoring and traffic signal adjustments are made possible by IoT sensors and data analytics. This shortens commute times and lessens traffic.

- **Public Safety:** Smart surveillance systems,

coordinated emergency response, and environmental monitoring for threats like water or air pollution are some of the ways that IoT improves public safety.

- **Sustainable Urban Development**: IoT helps to promote sustainability by optimizing resource management. Examples of this include smart waste management systems, smart water management systems, and smart power distribution networks.

2.3 Industrial Internet of Things - Improving Maintenance and Operations

The use of IoT technology in the industrial sector to boost productivity, safety, and operational efficiency is known as industrial IoT, or IIoT.

2.3.1 Predictive Maintenance:

- **Condition Monitoring:** Internet of Things (IoT) sensors continuously track the state of machinery and equipment, looking for wear indicators and any malfunctions before they happen. This minimizes downtime and enables prompt maintenance.
- **Data Analytics:** By processing sensor data,

sophisticated analytics systems forecast when maintenance should be done, streamlining schedules and cutting expenses.

2.3.2 Process Optimization:

- **Real-Time Monitoring:** IoT makes it possible to monitor industrial processes in real-time, allowing for quick adjustments to boost production and efficiency. For instance, sensors monitor production parameters in the manufacturing industry to guarantee quality control.

- **Automation:** IoT connects to industrial automation systems to improve operational accuracy and dependability. Human error can be decreased and production can be increased by using robotics and automated machinery to communicate and coordinate more efficiently.

2.3.3 Supply Chain Management:

- **Inventory Management:** Real-time inventory tracking is made possible by IoT sensors, which also help to prevent stockouts and overstock scenarios. This results in a supply chain that is more economical and efficient.

- **Logistics and Fleet Management:** Internet of Things gadgets track the whereabouts and state of cargo while in route, maximizing efficiency and guaranteeing on-time delivery. To improve efficiency and safety, fleet management systems monitor driver behavior and vehicle performance.

2.4 Privacy and Security Issues in the Linked World

Significant security and privacy issues are brought about by the IoT's widespread adoption, and these issues must be resolved to guarantee the secure and safe operation of linked devices.

2.4.1 Security Risks:

- **Data Breaches:** Because IoT devices gather and send enormous volumes of data, hackers find them to be appealing targets. To stop unwanted access, secure communication routes and data encryption are crucial.

- **Vulnerabilities in Devices:** Because many IoT devices have low RAM and computing power, it might be difficult to put strong security measures in place. Security must be given top priority by manufacturers when creating and designing these gadgets.

- **Network Security:** Since IoT devices frequently share a network with other vital systems, network security is extremely important. Risks can be reduced by putting robust network segmentation and access controls in place.

2.4.2 Privacy Concerns:

- **Data Collection:** Sensitive personal data, including location, usage patterns, and health information, is collected by IoT devices. Retaining trust requires getting user consent and being transparent about data gathering procedures.

- **Usage of Data:** Users want to know that their information will be handled appropriately and solely for those purposes. It is crucial to follow data protection laws like the GDPR and to have clear rules on the use of personal data.

- **Name-withholding:** By preventing easy reconnection of personal information to specific individuals, data anonymization techniques can help safeguard user privacy.

The Internet of Things is revolutionizing our world by facilitating device connectivity, streamlining processes, and improving quality of life. To guarantee the safe and ethical use of IoT technologies, security and privacy issues must be addressed. IoT will have a bigger impact on how our connected world develops in the future as it continues to advance.

CHAPTER 3

ANALYTICS AND BIG DATA: UNCOVERING SECRET KNOWLEDGE

3.1 Big Data's Power: Gathering, Preserving, and Handling Massive Datasets

Big Data is the term used to describe the massive amount of data that is produced every second by multiple sources, including social media, sensors, transactions, and more. When appropriately collected, saved, and processed, this data which is distinguished by its volume, velocity, diversity, and veracity has the ability to yield important insights and influence decision-making.

3.1.1 Gathering Big Data:

- **Data Sources:** Big Data can be gathered from a variety of sources, including as transactional systems, social media platforms, and Internet of Things devices. It is crucial to comprehend these sources in order to collect data effectively.

- **Data capture Tools:** Technologies like web scraping, APIs, and data streaming allow for the real-time or batch capture of big datasets. Examples include the web scraping tool Scrapy and the data streaming tool Apache Kafka.

3.1.2 Data Warehouses:

- **Big Data Storing:** Structured data from transactional systems is stored in traditional data warehouses. They offer strong analytics capabilities and make use of SQL databases.

- **Data Lakes:** Data lakes, as opposed to data warehouses, are capable of storing data at any scale, both structured and unstructured. Often, Hadoop and Amazon S3 are utilized in the construction of data lakes.

- **Systems of Distributed Storage:** Distributed storage systems like HDFS (Hadoop Distributed File System) and cloud storage solutions are used to assure scalability and dependability in handling the enormous volume of Big Data.

3.1.3 Big Data Processing:

- **Batch Processing:** Processes substantial data blocks in batches over an extended period of time. Spark and Apache Hadoop are well-liked frameworks for batch processing because of their effective handling of massive amounts of data.

- **Stream Processing:** Processes data streams in real-time to extract insights as they are generated. For stream processing, tools like Apache Kafka and Apache Flink are frequently utilized, which facilitates prompt decision-making.

- **ETL (Extract, Transform, Load):** Processes used in ETL are essential for converting unprocessed data into a format that can be used. These procedures are streamlined and automated by programs like Talend and Apache Nifi.

3.2 Data-Driven Decisions and Business Intelligence: Obtaining a Competitive Edge

Using big data and analytics to produce insights that can be put into practice and help with decision-making is known as business intelligence, or BI. Organizations can gain a competitive edge, comprehend trends, and spot opportunities with the use of BI tools and approaches.

3.2.1 Culture Driven by Data:

- **Data Usability:** It is essential to make sure decision-makers can quickly access data. Self-service BI tools, such as Tableau and Power BI, enable users to generate dashboards and reports without the need for IT support.

- **Intelligent Data:** Encouraging data literacy among staff members aids in their comprehension and efficient use of data. Workshops and training courses can improve data skills in a variety of departments.

3.2.2 BI Tools and Technologies:

- **Reporting Tools:** BI reporting tools like Microsoft Power BI, Tableau, and Looker enable the production of interactive reports and dashboards that provide a comprehensive picture of business indicators.

- **OLAP (Online Analytical Processing):** Complex analytical and ad hoc queries can be executed quickly with OLAP tools. They are necessary for business data multidimensional analysis.

- **Information Mining:** Techniques such as clustering, classification, and regression analysis are used to discover patterns and relationships in large datasets, enabling predictive analytics.

3.2.3 Competitive Advantage:

- **Market Analysis:** BI tools analyze market trends, customer preferences, and competitor actions, providing businesses with the insights needed to stay ahead of the competition.
- **Operational Efficiency:** By examining operational data, firms can find inefficiencies and areas for improvement, resulting in cost savings and better production.
- **consumer Insights:** Understanding consumer behavior and preferences through data analysis assists in personalizing marketing campaigns, enhancing customer satisfaction, and increasing loyalty.

3.3 Data Visualization: Transforming Statistics into Intriguing Tales

The graphical display of information and data is known as data visualization. By using visual elements like charts, graphs, and maps, data visualization tools give an accessible approach to observe and comprehend trends, outliers, and patterns in data.

3.3.1 Importance of Data Visualization:

- **Simplifies Complex Data:** Visualizations simplify complex datasets, making it easier for stakeholders to understand insights and make informed decisions.
- **Identifies Trends and Patterns:** Visual tools help in quickly identifying trends, correlations, and anomalies that might be missed in tabular data.
- **Engages Stakeholders:** Effective visualizations engage stakeholders by providing captivating data tales, promoting greater communication and cooperation.

3.3.2 Types of Data Visualizations:

- **Charts and Graphs:** Common types include bar charts, line graphs, pie charts, and scatter plots, each suited for different kinds of data analysis.

- **Heatmaps:** These visualizations represent data in matrix form, using color to represent values, making it easy to spot trends and correlations.

- **Geospatial Visualizations:** Maps and spatial data representations are used to visualize data across geographical locations, useful in logistics, retail, and public health analysis.

3.3.3 Visualization Tools:

- **Tableau:** Known for its sophisticated data visualization capabilities and ease of use, Tableau allows users to construct a wide range of interactive and shared dashboards.

- **Microsoft Power BI:** A versatile tool that connects with numerous data sources, giving comprehensive visualization and reporting features.

- **D3.js:** A JavaScript toolkit for producing unique data visualizations in web browsers, allowing for highly customizable and dynamic graphics.

3.4 Ethical Considerations of Big Data - Privacy and Discrimination

The use of Big Data creates substantial ethical considerations, particularly around privacy and potential discrimination. Addressing these concerns is vital to ensure the proper use of data and sustain public trust.

3.4.1 Privacy Concerns:

- **Data Collection:** Collecting enormous volumes of personal data can intrude on individual privacy. Organizations must guarantee transparent data gathering processes and acquire informed consent from users.
- **Data Security:** It's imperative to safeguard data against breaches and unauthorized access. Sensitive data is protected when strong security measures, such encryption and access limits, are put in place.
- **Name-withholding:** Data anonymization preserves individual identities while enabling insightful analysis. Re-identification risks, however, need to be handled cautiously.

3.4.2 Discrimination Risks:

- **Algorithmic Bias:** Discriminatory results may result from data or algorithmic bias. To maintain justice and equity, biases in data collecting and processing must be recognized and minimized.

- **Intelligent AI Methods:** Preventing discriminatory activities can be aided by creating and upholding ethical AI norms. Implementing AI ethically is aided by transparent algorithms and routine audits.

- **Compliance with Regulations:** Compliance with data protection laws, such the CCPA and GDPR, guarantees that businesses follow moral and legal guidelines around data use and privacy.

Big data and analytics can reveal obscure information that spurs creativity and gives businesses a competitive edge. To guarantee the proper use of data and uphold public confidence, it is imperative to address ethical issues. Organizations must remain alert in their efforts to use data responsibly and productively as the area develops.

CHAPTER 4

AUTOMATION AND ROBOTICS: THE EMERGENCE OF SENSIBLE MACHINES

4.1 Transitioning from Collaborative to Industrial Robots

Robotics has advanced significantly, moving from simple industrial robots to increasingly complex collaboration robots, or cobots. This development represents a substantial shift in the way robots carry out activities and interact with human workers.

4.1.1 Industrial Robots:

- **Characteristics:** Usually employed in manufacturing and production settings, industrial robots are sizable, stationary devices. They are made for repeated, high-speed jobs including material handling, welding, painting, and assembly.
- **Accuracy and Effectiveness:** These robots are very

good at precisely and efficiently completing jobs, which lowers human error and boosts output. They are frequently designed to function in extremely regulated settings.

- **Detachment from People:** Owing to their size and strength, industrial robots are typically used in remote locations or behind safety barriers to avoid mishaps. If improperly contained, these machines can be extremely dangerous to human workers.

4.1.2 Cobots (Collaborative Robots):

- **Features:** Cobots are intended to operate in a shared workspace with human employees. To ensure safe interactions with humans, they are more compact, versatile, and furnished with cutting-edge sensors and artificial intelligence.

- **Features for Safety:** Because of their force-limited joints, sensors, and sensitive control systems that enable them to recognize and respond to human presence, cobots are designed with safety in mind, lowering the possibility of harm.

- **Uses:** Cobots are employed in many different sectors, including logistics, healthcare, and manufacturing. They boost efficiency and free up human attention for more intricate and creative work by helping with jobs like assembly, quality control, and material management.

4.2 Automation in Various Industries: Healthcare, Manufacturing, and Other

Automation is improving services, cutting costs, and increasing efficiency across a number of industries. Different sectors embrace automation technologies in different ways, and each has its own advantages and applications.

4.2.1 Manufacturing:

- **Production Lines:** Robotics, conveyor systems, and automated guided vehicles (AGVs) are examples of automation used in manufacturing to optimize production lines. Faster manufacturing cycles, less waste, and better-quality products are the results of this.

- **Quality Control:** To identify flaws and guarantee product quality, automated technologies are utilized, such as machine vision and AI-based inspection tools. These technologies are significantly more capable than humans, analyzing thousands of products every minute.

- **Supply Chain Management:** Supply chain management automation uses sensors, IoT devices, and AI algorithms to track shipments, forecast demand, and optimize inventory levels. Supply networks become more robust and efficient as a result.

4.2.2 Healthcare:

- **Surgical Robots:** Surgeons can execute minimally invasive treatments with more control and precision thanks to robotic surgery devices like the da Vinci Surgical System. These devices shorten recuperation periods for patients and enhance surgical results.

- **Medical Attention:** Medication administration, assistive care, and patient monitoring are all done by automated systems. Medical supplies can be transported throughout hospitals by robots such as TUG, while telepresence robots allow for remote consultations and care.

- **Diagnostics:** Artificial intelligence and machine learning algorithms examine genetic and imaging data to help diagnose illnesses and suggest courses of action. Automated diagnostic tools improve healthcare delivery speed and accuracy.

4.2.3 Beyond Manufacturing and Healthcare:

- **Agriculture:** Drones, self-driving tractors, and robotic harvesters are examples of automation in agriculture. These innovations lower labor costs, boost yields, and enhance crop management.

- **Warehousing and Logistics:** Robots and AI are used in automated warehouses to handle inventory, complete orders, and streamline logistics processes. Robots are used by businesses like Amazon and Alibaba to automate warehouse operations.

- **Retail:** Self-checkout devices, AI-powered inventory control, and data analytics-driven individualized consumer experiences are examples of retail automation. Both operational effectiveness and consumer happiness are improved by these technologies.

4.3 Automation and the Human Workforce: The Future of Jobs

The labor force will be significantly impacted by the advent of automation and intelligent machinery. Automation changes jobs and opens up new opportunities, but it can also result in job displacement.

4.3.1 Workplace Relocation:

- **Daily Activities:** The majority of employment affected by automation involves repetitive, everyday tasks. Customer service, data entry, and manufacturing jobs are the ones most susceptible to automation.

- **Impact on the Economy:** Significant negative effects on the economy and society, such as higher unemployment rates and income inequality, can result from job relocation. Governments and organizations must address these issues by implementing programs and regulations that assist impacted workers.

4.3.2 Job Conversion:

- **Demand for Skills:** Demand for higher-skilled occupations requiring technical proficiency, creative problem-solving skills, and inventiveness alters as a result of automation. Employees must adjust by taking up lifelong learning and mastering new skills.

- **Partnership Between Humans and Robots:** Human-machine cooperation will be required in many jobs as robots and AI systems proliferate. Because of this, employees must learn how to operate and communicate with automated systems.

4.3.3 Creation of Jobs:

- **New Sectors:** New industries and professional roles particularly in technology, artificial intelligence, and robotics are being driven by automation. Data science, cybersecurity, and AI development are three areas that are expanding quickly.

- **Aiding Services:** There are more career opportunities created by automated system administration, programming, and maintenance. Effective automation technology adoption requires roles in IT services, system integration, and technical support.

4.4 Safety, Accountability, and Human Interaction as Ethical Considerations for Robotics

There are significant ethical questions raised by the societal integration of automation and robotics. For these technologies to evolve sustainably and be accepted, it is imperative that they be used in a responsible, ethical, and safe manner.

4.4.1 Security:

- **Construction and Guidelines:** Safety must be the top consideration in the design of robots. Respecting global safety guidelines, including ISO 10218 for industrial robots, can reduce hazards and guarantee secure operations.

- **Compliance and Regulation:** Regulations and standards for the safe use of automated systems and robots are primarily set by governments and regulatory agencies. To enforce these standards, routine inspections and compliance checks are required.

4.4.2 Accountability:

- **Responsibility:** Determining who is responsible for a robot-related malfunction or accident is a complicated matter. To resolve liability problems, obligations must be explicitly defined by manufacturers, operators, and users.

- **AI Ethics:** Ensuring openness, fairness, and bias mitigation in AI algorithms is essential to developing ethical AI. To guarantee ethical AI practices, organizations need to put ethical rules into place and carry out frequent audits.

4.4.3 Interaction with Humans:

- **Social Implications:** The rising pervasiveness of robots in daily life has an impact on social dynamics and human interactions. It is crucial to make sure that robots are made to facilitate human interactions rather than obstruct them.

- **Effects on Emotion and Psychology:** There are concerns over the emotional and psychological toll that using robots in companionship and caregiving jobs will have on people. It's critical to strike a balance between the advantages of robotic help and the requirement for real human interactions.

The emergence of robotics and automation is changing labor markets, upending businesses, and posing significant ethical questions. To guarantee that these technologies have a good influence on society as they develop further, it is imperative to address issues of safety, accountability, and human connection. We can utilize the full potential of intelligent machines to make our planet a better place if we accept these developments with consideration and responsibility.

CHAPTER 5

VIRTUAL AND AUGMENTED REALITY'S RISE AND ITS POTENTIAL TO RESHAPE REALITY

5.1 Immersion in Virtual Reality: Applications and Experiences

Through the creation of a fully immersive digital environment, virtual reality (VR) enables users to interact and experience a simulated world much like they would in real life. With the help of this technology, we can now interact with digital content in ways that were previously unthinkable.

5.1.1 Immersion Experiences

- **Entire-Body Immersion:** Head-mounted displays and motion tracking are used by VR systems like the Oculus Rift, HTC Vive, and PlayStation VR to deliver a 360-degree perspective and a sensation of presence in a virtual environment. Haptic feedback devices and motion platforms are examples of advanced setups that improve physical experiences.

- **Sensual Interaction:** Sight, hearing, and touch are just a few of the senses that virtual reality (VR) uses to create a realistic virtual experience. For instance, spatial audio technology increases the realism of the experience by enabling users to sense sound directionally.

- **Intelligent Settings:** Hand controls, gloves, or full-body suits allow users to engage with the virtual environment, facilitating complicated simulations, artistic production, and virtual sports. The immersive quality of virtual reality is largely due to this interaction.

5.1.2 VR Applications:

- **Entertainment and Gaming:** By enabling users to enter their favorite games and experience them firsthand, virtual reality gaming brings an all-new degree of immersion and engagement to the gaming experience. VR is utilized for immersive storytelling in movies and virtual concerts in addition to games.

- **Medicine:** Through the use of virtual reality,

medical students can practice procedures in a risk-free setting. Additionally, it helps with pain management, rehabilitation exercises for patients, and therapy like exposure therapy for phobias.

- **Architecture and Real Estate:** Through virtual reality (VR), clients can explore locations before they are developed by taking virtual tours of properties and architectural concepts. This facilitates decision-making with knowledge and real-time visualization of changes.

5.2 Using AR to Enhance Our World

By superimposing digital data over the actual world, augmented reality (AR) improves our view of and interactions with our surroundings. With AR, digital elements are integrated into our physical surroundings, as opposed to VR, which creates an entirely virtual experience.

5.2.1 Enhancing Reality:

- **Visual Overlays:** AR technology allows users to superimpose digital content, animations, and images onto the real world using gadgets like tablets, smartphones, and AR glasses. Apps like Pokémon GO and Google Maps' augmented reality navigation are two examples.

- **Contextual Information:** AR gives users access to real-time data based on their immediate environment. AR apps, for example, can reveal product details in a store, translate text on signs, and display information about landmarks.

- **Interactive Elements:** Augmented reality enables users to engage with virtual things inside their surroundings. This can involve interacting with interactive advertisements, playing AR games, or modifying 3D models.

5.2.2 AR Applications:

- **Education:** AR makes textbooks come to life with interactive 3D models, animations, and simulations. This improves learning. When on field tours or museum visits, it can also offer historical reconstructions and translations in real time.

- **Retail:** Thanks to AR, shopping is being revolutionized by the ability to virtually try on clothing, accessories, and makeup. The ability to preview things before buying them enhances the purchasing experience for customers.

- **Upkeep and Fixing:** With AR, technicians may do intricate jobs more easily by superimposing blueprints and instructions on their equipment. This lowers errors and boosts productivity in industries like machinery maintenance and auto repair.

5.3 VR/AR's Effect on the Education, Training, and Entertainment Sectors

Virtual reality (VR) and augmented reality (AR) are revolutionizing a number of industries by improving training, education, and entertainment. These technologies are providing creative solutions for a variety of industries while also transforming conventional approaches.

5.3.1 Education:

- **Immersive Learning:** Virtual reality (VR) offers immersive educational experiences that improve comprehension and retention by letting students explore historical locations, journey through space, or delve into the human body. AR enhances traditional education by adding interactive components that simplify difficult ideas.

- **Online Courses:** With the use of virtual reality (VR), students may attend lectures, work together on projects, and take part in conversations online from anywhere in the world. This is especially advantageous for international education and remote learning.

5.3.2 Instruction:

- **Virtual Settings:** VR training simulations provide a secure and regulated setting for practicing high-risk activities, like flight simulations, military maneuvers, and medical operations. These virtual experiences enhance abilities and readiness without the repercussions of actual errors.

- **Training on the Job:** AR supports and guides on-the-job trainees in real-time. Field technicians, for instance, can solve issues and get step-by-step instructions using AR glasses, all without consulting manuals or superiors.

5.3.3 Entertainment:

- **Immersive Storytelling:** Thanks to virtual reality and augmented reality, immersive storytelling experiences in theaters, movies, and theme parks are revolutionizing the entertainment sector. By engaging with characters and exploring virtual places, viewers can immerse themselves in the narrative.

- **In-person Events:** By offering interactive features and real-time information, augmented reality (AR) improves live events like concerts and sporting events. The viewing experience is enhanced by the availability of player statistics, immediate replays, and virtual meet-and-greets for fans.

5.4 VR/AR's Ethical Considerations: Addiction, Privacy, and Reality Blurring

The ethical implications of using VR and AR technologies must be addressed as they become more widely used. Careful management of issues like addiction, privacy, and reality distortion is necessary to guarantee the responsible and advantageous use of these technologies.

5.4.1 Compulsive Behavior:

- **Deep Escape:** Because VR is so engrossing, users may become addicted to it and come to favor virtual encounters over real-world ones. This may lead to detrimental effects on mental health, social isolation, and responsibility neglect.

- **Guidelines for Usage**: Setting limits for responsible VR use that encourage moderation and balance is essential. Together, developers and legislators can raise knowledge of the possible hazards and promote safe use.

5.4.2 Privacy:

- **Data Collection:** Location, camera, and microphone inputs are only a few examples of the personal data that AR apps frequently need access to. Data privacy and the possible misuse of sensitive information are brought up by this.

- **Policy and Protection:** To ensure user privacy, strong data protection laws and security measures must be put in place. Users ought to be in charge of their data and aware of how it's shared and utilized.

5.4.3 Reality Blurring:

- **Reality Perception:** Confusion and distorted views of reality might result from the blurring of the boundaries between the virtual and physical worlds. For younger users and those with pre-existing mental health disorders, this is especially troubling.

- **Design with Ethics:** When creating VR and AR experiences, developers need to take into account the psychological repercussions of their work and make sure that their designs are morally sound and user-centered. It can be helpful to reduce these dangers to establish distinct boundaries between virtual and real worlds.

Virtual reality (VR) and augmented reality (AR) technologies are transforming how we interact with digital material by providing immersive and engaging experiences that improve a variety of sectors. To guarantee their appropriate and advantageous deployment, it is imperative to address the ethical issues surrounding their use. Through comprehension and effective handling of these obstacles, we may fully utilize VR and AR to transform our world in a constructive manner.

CHAPTER 6

6.1 Algorithmic Misconduct's Basis: Data Bias

Data quality and representativeness are vital because AI systems learn from it. When historical preconceptions or a lack of diversity are reflected in the datasets used to train AI models, data bias results in distorted outputs.

6.1.1 Data Bias Sources:

- **Historical Inequalities:** Data frequently reflects the prejudices held by society at the time of collecting. For instance, racial or gender prejudices from previous hiring practices may be inherited by a hiring algorithm based on historical employment data.

- **Income Bias:** Biased results may result from a dataset that is not representative of the population it is intended to serve. For example, an AI model that was mostly trained on urban data could not function effectively in rural settings.

- **Information Bias:** This happens when the process of gathering data contains errors or inconsistencies. One way to add bias is to use proxy variables, which may not precisely convey the intended concept.

6.1.2 Data Bias Consequences:

Skewed Predictions: Predictions made by AI models for particular groups may be erroneous due to biased data. For instance, individuals with darker skin tones may experience higher error rates in facial recognition systems.

Standardization of Stereotypes: Preconceived notions can be strengthened by biased datasets, which exacerbates societal injustices. Biased language models, for example, may produce literature that reinforces racial or gender prejudices.

6.2 Algorithmic Bias: How Inequality Is Maintained by Algorithms

Algorithms can induce or magnify biases through their design and execution, even with unbiased data. Decisions made throughout the model-building process, such as the attributes that are prioritized and how the data is handled, can lead to algorithmic bias.

6.2.1 Sources of Algorithmic Bias:

- **Feature Selection:** Choosing which characteristics to include in a model might cause bias. This is one of the Sources of Algorithmic Bias. For instance, racial biases may be unintentionally encoded when using zip codes as a stand-in for socioeconomic status.

- **Model Training:** Predictions may be biased as a result of algorithms overfitting to biased patterns in the training set. To reduce this risk, strategies like cross-validation and regularization are crucial.

- **Feedback Loops:** Biases may be amplified by feedback loops produced by AI systems that are always learning from their own forecasts. Recommendation systems, for instance, have the potential to reinforce preexisting preferences and limit exposure to a variety of content.

6.2.2 Algorithmic Bias Examples:

- **Hiring Algorithms:** AI that is used in hiring may reinforce prejudices if it is trained on past data that shows underrepresentation of particular groups. Hiring practices that are biased may arise from this.

- **Policy Predictiveness:** If law enforcement algorithms are trained on skewed crime data, they may disproportionately target minority populations, resulting in unfair treatment and over policing.

6.3 The Effect of Bias: Inequitable Results and Injustice

In the real world, bias in AI systems can have a big impact on people and communities in a lot of different areas, such as criminal justice, healthcare, and finance.

6.3.1 Medical Care:

- **Inequalities in Therapy:** Unfair access to medical care might result from biased algorithms in the healthcare industry. For instance, insufficient treatment may come from an AI model that overestimates the risk of disease for specific demographics.

- **Medical Insurance:** Predictive models that health insurers utilize may be biased, which could result in unjust premium rates or coverage choices that disproportionately impact underprivileged populations.

6.3.2 Finance:

- **Credit Scoring:** Injustices in lending practices may arise from bias in credit scoring algorithms. Biased credit evaluations may result in loans to minority groups being refused or having unfavorable terms given.
- **Identifying Fraud:** Fraud detection systems that exhibit bias may cause increased false positive rates for specific groups, which could lead to unwarranted account freezes or denials of service.

6.3.3 Criminal Justice:

- **sentence and Parole:** Decisions about sentence and parole can be influenced by bias in risk assessment instruments employed in the criminal justice system, which can result in outcomes that are disproportionately harsher for minority groups.

- **Policy Predictiveness:** As has already been established, biased algorithms have the potential to exacerbate already-existing socioeconomic inequalities by over policing particular communities.

6.4 Identifying Algorithmic Bias and Recognizing Bias - Methods

It is crucial to identify and comprehend AI bias in order to address it. A variety of methods and approaches can be used to detect and reduce bias in AI systems.

6.4.1 Fairness Metrics:

- **Demographic Parity:** This statistic guarantees homogeneity of the decision rate among various demographic subgroups. An equitable rate of selection of candidates from diverse genders should be ensured via a recruiting algorithm.

- **Standardized Odds:** For this measure to be used, all demographic groups must have equal false positive and false negative rates. This guarantees that no group is disproportionately impacted by the model's error rates.

- **Adjustment:** Regardless of the demographic group, a model is considered calibrated if the predicted probabilities accurately represent the likelihood of an event occurring. For instance, an AI's prediction of a 70% likelihood of loan repayment ought to apply to all demographic categories.

6.4.2 Recommendations for Bias Detection Tools:

Algorithm Reviews: Frequent reviews of AI systems might reveal biases. Examining the data, methods, and results is what audits entail in order to guarantee transparency and equity.

Bias Rewards: Bias rewards encourage researchers and practitioners to find and report biases in AI systems, much like bug bounties do in cybersecurity.

Explainability Tools: By assisting in the understanding of the decision-making process of AI models, tools such as SHAP (SHapley Additive exPlanations) and LIME (Local Interpretable Model-agnostic Explanations) facilitate the identification and remediation of biases.

6.4.3 Diverse Information and Groups:

- **Comprehensive Datasets:** Bias can be decreased by making sure the training data is representative and diverse. Data collection from a range of demographic groups should be attempted, and historical biases should be avoided.

- **Multicultural Development Teams:** AI system development teams ought to be inclusive and varied. Several viewpoints can be useful in spotting possible biases and guaranteeing impartial results.

Developing just and equitable AI systems requires an understanding of and response to AI bias. We can develop AI that equitably serves all people and communities by understanding the causes and effects of bias and using strategies to detect and reduce it.

CHAPTER 7

FAIRER ALGORITHMS AND AI BIAS MITIGATION TECHNIQUES

7.1 Inclusive Data Gathering - Guaranteeing Diversity and Representation

The foundation for developing impartial and equitable AI systems is inclusive data collection. It is possible to reduce the possibility of biased results and advance justice in AI-driven decision-making by making sure that the data is representative of many communities.

7.1.1 Essential Elements of Inclusive Data Gathering:

- **Representation:** Gather information from a wide range of demographics to guarantee that every group is fairly represented. This entails taking into account elements including ethnicity, gender, age, socioeconomic position, and geography.
- **Diversity:** To capture a wide range of experiences and opinions, incorporate a variety of data sources

and types. This method assists in producing a comprehensive dataset that lowers the possibility of bias.

- **previous Context:** Identify and correct previous biases in the data that is currently available. This entails evaluating data sources thoroughly and making necessary adjustments to make sure they don't reinforce historical biases.

7.1.2 Techniques for Putting Inclusive Data Collection into Practice:

- **Data Audits:** Conduct regular dataset audits to find and close any representational gaps. To do this, a demographic balance analysis of the data must be performed to make sure no group is substantially underrepresented.

- **Collaborative Data Sourcing:** Work with stakeholders and a range of communities to collect data that represents a range of experiences. Partnerships with groups that represent various demographic groupings may fall under this category.

- **Continuous Monitoring:** Put in place continuing monitoring systems to guarantee that data holds true throughout time. This entails routinely updating datasets to account for shifts in the population's makeup.

7.2 Algorithmic Fairness Methods: Reducing Prejudice in Development and Design

In order to create AI systems that reduce prejudice and advance equal results, algorithmic fairness techniques are crucial. The goal of these methods is to make sure that algorithms don't unfairly disfavor any one group.

7.2.1 Algorithmic Fairness Methods:

- **Fairness Restrictions:** When designing the algorithm, take fairness limitations into consideration. These limitations guarantee that the algorithm's forecasts are fair to all demographic categories.

- **Methods for Mitigating Biases:** Employ bias mitigation techniques that adapt the training data to any identified biases. Reweighting, oversampling, and undersampling are a few methods that can be used to balance the data and lessen bias.

- **Adversarial Debiasing:** Use adversarial training strategies in which biases in the primary model are identified and reduced using an opponent, a secondary model.

7.2.2 Bias Mitigation Techniques:

- **Pre-processing Techniques:** Adjust training data before the algorithm feed to remove biases. This can involve methods such as feature selection, data standardization, and data augmentation.

- **In-processing Techniques:** Modify the algorithm's learning procedure to reduce bias. In order to do this, during model training, fairness constraints must be directly incorporated into the optimization target.

- **Post-processing Techniques:** Adjust the algorithm's outputs to guarantee equitable results. Techniques such as equalized odds post-processing, which modifies the algorithm's predictions to attain equity among various groups, can be included in this.

7.3 Transparency in AI Decisions: Human Oversight and Explainability

Explainability and human monitoring are essential elements of moral AI. We can assure responsibility and trust in AI systems by making AI judgments clear and visible.

7.3.1 The Significance of Human Oversight:

- **Accountability:** Human oversight guarantees that judgments made using AI are held accountable. When AI systems make incorrect or biased conclusions, humans can step in to correct them.

- **Ethical Evaluation**: Ethical considerations that AI systems might miss are made possible by human monitoring. People are capable of making complex choices that take moral considerations and circumstances into account.

7.3.2 Methods for Improving Explainability:

- **Model Interpretability:** Create AI models, like decision trees or linear models, that are naturally interpretable. These models offer lucid insights into the decision-making process.

- **Methods for Post-hoc Explainability:** To describe complex models, employ strategies such as SHAP (SHapley Additive exPlanations) and LIME (Local Interpretable Model-agnostic Explanations). These techniques shed light on how each feature affects the final prediction.

- **Accounts of Transparency:** Provide reports on openness that explain how AI systems make decisions. The data that were used, the behavior of the model, and any biases that were found should all be covered in these reports.

7.3.3 Establishing Robust Human Oversight:

- **AI Ethics Committees:** Form committees to supervise the creation and application of AI systems. In order to provide thorough monitoring, these committees must comprise a variety of stakeholders.

- **Ongoing Surveillance:** Establish ongoing monitoring systems to keep tabs on AI system performance. To find and fix any biases or ethical issues, this entails routine audits and reviews.

- **Feedback Loops:** Provide feedback loops so that people can voice concerns about AI judgments. User comments might offer insightful information about possible biases and areas in need of development.

7.4 Legal Frameworks: Creating Guidelines for Ethical AI

Establishing norms and regulations for the creation and use of moral AI requires regulatory frameworks. These frameworks guarantee that AI systems are created ethically and that society norms and values are upheld when using them.

7.4.1 Elements of Successful Regulatory Frameworks:

- **Legal Standards:** Clearly define the legal parameters for the creation and application of AI. These guidelines ought to cover matters like accountability, bias mitigation, and data privacy.
- **Ethical Guidelines:** Formulate moral standards that offer a foundation for conscientious AI development. The aforementioned standards ought to prioritize equity, openness, and observance of human rights.

- **Compliance processes:** In order to ensure that regulatory standards are followed, put compliance processes in place. Regular audits, certifications, and sanctions for non-compliance are all part of this.

The General Data Protection Regulation (GDPR):

- **Examples of Regulatory Frameworks:** A thorough framework for data privacy and protection in the EU is offered by the GDPR. It contains clauses pertaining to responsibility, data reduction, and openness.

- **The Algorithmic Accountability Act:** A bill that has been proposed in the US to force businesses to assess their AI systems for discrimination, bias, and other moral issues.

- **The IEEE Global effort on Ethics of Autonomous and Intelligent Systems:** This effort, which prioritizes responsibility, transparency, and the welfare of people, offers standards for the moral development and application of AI systems.

7.4.3 Putting Regulatory Frameworks into Practice:

- **Policy Development:** Collaborate with legislators, business leaders, and civil society organizations to create thorough regulatory frameworks. This cooperative method guarantees that many viewpoints are taken into account.

- **Standardization Bodies:** Form standardization organizations to define and uphold technical guidelines for the advancement of artificial intelligence. To achieve broad applicability, these groups should include members from many sectors.

- **International Cooperation:** Encourage international cooperation to standardize AI laws among various legal systems. This guarantees that AI systems created in one area follow global ethical norms.

A complex strategy that includes inclusive data gathering, algorithmic fairness methods, human oversight, and strong regulatory frameworks is needed to mitigate AI prejudice. By putting these tactics into practice, we may create AI systems that are equitable, open, and consistent with moral standards, eventually fostering justice and confidence in

AI-driven judgments.

CHAPTER 8

AI ETHICS IN THE FUTURE: CREATING A RESPONSIBLY DESIGNED FUTURE

8.1 Teamwork and Communication - Promoting a Free and Honest Discussion on AI Ethics

Artificial intelligence (AI) development and application require a cooperative strategy that brings together a variety of stakeholders to talk about and resolve ethical issues. To guarantee that AI technologies are developed ethically and in line with society norms, open discourse is important.

8.1.1 Crucial Components of Cooperation and Communication:

- **Multi-Stakeholder Involvement:** Involve a range of stakeholders, such as the public, policymakers, technologists, and ethicists. A comprehensive approach to tackling ethical concerns requires the distinct viewpoints and knowledge that each group brings to the table.

- **Interdisciplinary Approach:** Encourage cooperation between experts in various fields, including law, sociology, computer science, and philosophy. This guarantees a comprehensive comprehension of the ethical consequences associated with AI.

- **Ongoing Dialogue:** Create avenues of communication to address changing ethical issues. Frequent conferences, workshops, and forums can help to promote ongoing communication and knowledge exchange.

8.1.2 Techniques for Productive Cooperation and Communication:

- **Ethics Committees:** Establish ethics committees within companies to supervise AI development and guarantee ethical issues are taken into account right away. Diverse backgrounds should be represented on these committees.

- **Public Forums:** To get community feedback, schedule town hall meetings and public forums. This facilitates comprehending public concerns and applying them to AI practices and policies.

- **Transparency Projects:** By disclosing details about data sources, algorithms, and decision-making procedures, AI initiatives can be made more transparent. Openness fosters trust and makes it easier to have knowledgeable conversations regarding AI ethics.

8.2 Public Education and Awareness: Comprehending AI's Consequences

Building an informed society that can have meaningful conversations and make well-informed judgments regarding AI technology requires educating the public about AI and its ethical implications.

8.2.1 Public Education and Awareness:

- **Informed Decision-Making:** Knowledgeable people are better able to make decisions on the application and control of artificial intelligence (AI) technology.
- **Public Confidence:** Public acceptance and trust can be increased by educating people about the

advantages and dangers of AI. For AI to be successfully used in a variety of domains, trust is necessary.

- **Empowerment:** People who get public education are better able to advocate for ethical AI practices and take part in conversations on AI ethics.

8.2.2 Methods for Raising Public Awareness and Education:

- **Educational Campaigns:** Start educational campaigns that use understandable language to describe AI concepts, applications, and ethical dilemmas. Reach a large audience by using a variety of media platforms, such as social media.

- **Educational Programs:** Include ethical considerations for AI in school curricula to start teaching the future generation about the ramifications of AI at a young age. Courses in computer science, ethics, and social studies may fall under this category.

- **Public Workshops:** Arrange seminars and workshops for various societal groups. These seminars can offer practical learning opportunities and promote a greater comprehension of AI ethics.

8.3 Policy Makers' Role in Establishing Standards for Ethical AI Development

The establishment of rules and regulations by policymakers is essential to ensuring that AI technologies are created and used properly. Ethical issues can be resolved and the public interest advanced by effective policy.

8.3.1 Key Duties of Policymakers:

- **Supervision and Regulation:** Formulate and implement rules addressing moral concerns including data privacy, bias, and responsibility in AI systems. Laws should change to keep up with the quick speed at which technology is developing.
- **Funding and Support:** Give research on AI ethics funding and support. This covers financing for public education campaigns in addition to grants for scholarly study.
- **Stakeholder Engagement:** Actively interact with different sector stakeholders to get their opinions and develop a consensus on AI policies. This cooperative

approach guarantees that policies are generally approved and well-informed.

8.3.2 Techniques for Successful Policy Development:

- **Inclusive Policy-Making:** Include a variety of stakeholders in the policy-making process to guarantee that various viewpoints are taken into account. Working groups, advisory panels, and public consultations can help promote inclusive policy formulation.

- **Dynamic Regulations:** Construct adaptable rules that can be modified in response to advancements in AI technology. This guarantees that policies continue to be applicable and efficient in tackling novel ethical dilemmas.

- **Global Standards:** Seek to create international guidelines on AI morality. International collaboration can assist in preventing ethical differences between nations and harmonizing rules.

8.4 Global Collaboration - Handling AI Ethics' Global Challenges

Global in scope, AI technologies have ethical ramifications that cut beyond national borders. In order to solve the worldwide issues surrounding AI ethics and guarantee that AI advances mankind as a whole, international cooperation is crucial.

8.4.1 Importance of International Cooperation:

- **worldwide Standards:** Creating worldwide guidelines for AI ethics can guarantee equity and uniformity in the creation and application of AI in many nations.
- **Common Files:** Countries can exchange best practices, resources, and information through international collaboration. This could hasten the creation of moral AI and more successfully handle shared problems.
- **Taking Care of Cross-Border Concerns:** Numerous ethical concerns surrounding artificial intelligence, like cybersecurity and data privacy, are

international in scope. A comprehensive approach to tackling these concerns requires international cooperation.

8.4.2 International Cooperation Mechanisms:

- **International Treaties:** Formulate international treaties and accords outlining common ethical norms and guidelines for artificial intelligence. These contracts may offer a structure for responsibility and cooperation.

- **International Forums:** Take part in international forums and organizations devoted to AI ethics, like the IEEE Global Initiative on Ethics of Autonomous and Intelligent Systems and the OECD's AI Policy Observatory. These forums encourage international communication and cooperation.

- **Collaborative Research:** Encourage joint research projects with scientists from many nations. Collaborative research initiatives might utilize varied specialties and viewpoints to tackle intricate moral quandaries.

8.4.3 Opportunities and Challenges:

- **Cultural Differences:** Ethical standards and cultural norms can differ among nations. Finding common ground and resolving these disagreements presents both a big challenge and a chance for growth and learning from one another.

- **Resource Disparities:** Different nations have different capacities and resources. International cooperation may ensure that all nations benefit from AI developments and help close these gaps.

- **Establishing Trust:** Establishing trust between nations is a prerequisite for productive cooperation. Building trust and cooperation requires open communication, respect for one another, and common objectives.

Coordinated efforts across all areas are needed to create a responsible AI future. An ethical AI ecosystem must include proactive policymaking, public education and awareness campaigns, stakeholder collaboration and communication, and international cooperation. By adopting these tactics, we may make the most of AI's revolutionary potential while making sure it complies with our moral principles and advances humankind as a whole.

CHAPTER 9

AI AND HUMAN RIGHTS: SAFEGUARDING ESSENTIAL LIBERTIES

9.1 Discrimination and Algorithmic Bias: Dangers to Human Rights

Human rights are seriously threatened by prejudice and bias resulting from algorithms. These prejudices have the power to maintain inequality and lead to unequal treatment, eroding the fundamental liberties that are essential to a just society.

9.1.1 Understanding Algorithmic Bias:

- **Definition and Causes:** When artificial intelligence (AI) systems generate biased or erroneous results, this is known as algorithmic bias. The lack of diversity in the development teams, imbalanced data gathering procedures, and biased training data are some of the causes.

- **Kinds of Prejudice:** Bias can be contextual (e.g.,

regional, socioeconomic) or demographic (e.g., race, gender, age). Each kind influences decision-making in a different way and has the potential to treat people or groups unfairly.

9.1.2 Algorithmic Discrimination Examples:

- **Criminal Justice:** Predictive policing algorithms may unfairly target minority communities, resulting in an overabundance of police presence and unfair court decisions.

- **Employment and Hiring:** AI-powered hiring technologies may unjustly give preference to some applicants over others on the basis of skewed standards, which could have an impact on the employment prospects of disadvantaged groups.

- **Credit Scoring:** People from economically disadvantaged backgrounds or those with lower credit ratings may be subject to discrimination by financial algorithms, which could affect their ability to obtain loans and other financial services.

9.1.3 Handling Algorithmic prejudice:

- **Diverse Data Gathering:** Make sure that the data utilized for algorithm training is inclusive of a range of demographics in order to minimize prejudice.

- **Baisaudits:** To detect and reduce biases, regularly audit AI systems. Employ methods and instruments to identify and fix algorithmic bias.

- **Inclusive Design:** In order to address potential biases from the outset, incorporate a variety of perspectives into the design and development of AI systems.

9.2 Security and Privacy Issues: Making Sure AI Systems Protect Data

Since AI systems routinely manage enormous volumes of sensitive and personal data, privacy and security considerations are critical. Maintaining data security is essential to defending human rights.

9.2.1 Concerns Regarding Data Privacy:

- **Collection and Use of Data:** AI systems routinely gather, store, and process personal data, which, if improperly managed, can result in privacy violations. Knowing how data is gathered, utilized, and shared is crucial.

- **Informed Consent and Openness:** People should provide their agreement to the use of their data and be informed about the procedures used to gather it. Establishing transparency in the management of data fosters confidence and guarantees adherence to privacy laws.

9.2.2 Cybersecurity Risks:

- **Data Security Challenges:** Cybersecurity risks like data breaches and hacking can affect AI systems. Preserving data security requires safeguarding AI systems against these kinds of threats.
- **Data Security:** To protect data while it's in transit and at rest, use robust encryption procedures. Encryption guarantees data integrity and aids in preventing unwanted access.

9.2.3 Techniques for Safeguarding Security and Privacy:

- **Minimization of Data:** Gather only the information

required to run the AI system. The likelihood of privacy infractions is decreased by minimizing data collecting.

- **Anonymization:** When managing and analyzing data, use data anonymization procedures to safeguard people's identity. Anonymization reduces the threats to privacy.

- **Compliance with Regulations:** Respect data privacy laws including the California Consumer Privacy Act (CCPA) and the General Data Protection Regulation (GDPR). Ensuring compliance guarantees adherence to security and privacy regulations.

9.3 The Right to Clarification - Comprehending the Process of AI Decision Making

In the context of AI, one of the most important aspects of human rights is the right to explanation. It requires comprehending how AI systems arrive at judgments that have an impact on people's lives.

9.3.1 Significance of the Right to Clarification:

- **Accountability:** People have a right to know why judgments made by AI systems impact their chances and rights. They also have a right to know the reasoning behind those decisions.

- **Transparency and Trust:** Giving explanations promotes transparency and increases confidence in AI systems. It guarantees that judgments are reasonable and fair and lets people know how they are made.

9.3.2 Methods for Guaranteeing the Right to Explanation:

- **Explainable AI (XAI):** Create AI systems that provide comprehensible and intelligible justifications for their choices. Among the methods are rule-based systems, decision trees, and model behavior visualizations.

- **User-Friendly Interfaces:** Create user interfaces that provide explanations in a way that is easy for users to understand. Technical jargon should be avoided in favor of explanations that are clear and understandable.

- **Feedback Mechanisms:** Put in place ways for users to comment on the choices and justifications made by AI. This guarantees that explanations fulfill the demands of consumers and helps pinpoint areas that require improvement.

9.3.3 Difficulties and Resolutions:

- **Intricacy of Models:** Intricate artificial intelligence models, such deep learning networks, can be challenging to comprehend. Methods for deciphering and elucidating these models are still being researched.

- **Keeping Privacy and Transparency in Check:** Make sure that explanations don't jeopardize security or privacy. Make an effort to shield sensitive information while offering insightful explanations.

9.4 Encouraging AI that is Human-Centric: Giving Human Values Priority in Technology

Prioritizing human values and making sure AI technologies work best for people and society at large are key components of fostering human-centric AI.

9.4.1 Human-Centric AI Principles:

- **Respect for Human Dignity:** AI systems ought to be created with human dignity in mind and upheld accordingly. This entails preventing harm and encouraging favorable results for people.

- **Beneficence:** Make sure AI technologies advance people's welfare as well as the welfare of society. Put your energy into developing solutions that improve people's quality of life and deal with societal issues.

- **Autonomy:** Foster people's independence by creating AI systems that respect and empower users' decisions.

9.4.2 Techniques for Putting Human-Centric AI into Practice:

- **Ethical Design:** Include ethical issues in the planning and creation of AI systems. Collaborate with social scientists, ethicists, and interested parties to recognize and handle possible ethical dilemmas.

- **User-Centered Development:** Include users in the process of developing AI systems to make sure they fulfill their needs and are consistent with their values. Utilize methods of participatory design to get opinions and suggestions.

- **Impact Evaluations:** Evaluate the influence of AI systems on people and society by conducting impact evaluations on a regular basis. Make sure AI technologies are in line with human values by using these evaluations as a roadmap for future developments.

9.4.3 Opportunities and Challenges:

- **Balancing Innovation and Ethics:** Make an effort to strike a balance between ethical issues and technological innovation. Make sure moral standards are upheld while expanding the capabilities of AI.

- **Differences in Context and Culture:** Understand that human values can differ depending on the society and setting. Create AI systems with flexibility and sensitivity to a range of standards and values.

Tackling algorithmic prejudice, guaranteeing data privacy and security, respecting the right to explanation, and promoting human-centric AI are all necessary to defend fundamental freedoms in the context of AI. We can create AI systems that uphold human rights, advance justice, and benefit society by concentrating on these areas.

CHAPTER 10

AN AI-POWERED FUTURE: CREATING A BETTER TOMORROW

10.1 AI for Good: Applying AI to Advance Sustainability and Social Progress

Through addressing global issues and enhancing quality of life, artificial intelligence (AI) has the potential to significantly advance sustainability and social progress.

10.1.1 Artificial Intelligence for Social Impact:

- **Medical Advances:** Through effective medication discovery, tailored treatment regimens, and predictive diagnostics, artificial intelligence is revolutionizing healthcare. AI systems, for instance, are capable of analyzing medical imagery to more accurately and early identify ailments.

- **Improving Education:** Personalized learning experiences, adaptive tutoring systems, and support for a range of learning needs are provided by

AI-powered educational solutions. These resources, which are customized for each student, can aid in closing educational gaps.

- **Reaction to the Disaster**: Through data analysis to anticipate natural catastrophes, manage emergency services, and optimize resource allocation during crises, artificial intelligence (AI) can enhance disaster response and recovery efforts.

10.1.2 Artificial Intelligence for Environmental Sustainability:

- **climatic Change Mitigation:** AI models are able to monitor deforestation, forecast climatic patterns, and maximize the use of renewable energy. These apps support the creation of plans for managing natural resources and lowering carbon footprints.

- **Waste Management:** By classifying materials more effectively and forecasting trends of waste formation, AI systems can improve recycling procedures and waste management. This encourages recycling activities and lessens the amount of waste dumped in landfills.

- **Biodiversity Conservation:** AI systems support

tracking wildlife movements, keeping an eye on endangered species, and stopping poaching. These initiatives promote ecosystem health and biodiversity protection.

10.1.3 Encouraging Ethical AI Use:

- **Transparency:** Make sure that the goals, processes, and effects of AI systems deployed for social and environmental reasons are openly disclosed. Accountability and trust are fostered by transparency.

- **Participate with Stakeholders:** Involve communities and experts with the development and application of AI solutions. Including a range of viewpoints ensures that pertinent social and environmental issues are adequately addressed by AI applications.

10.2 The Value of AI and Human Collaboration: Using Both of Their Potential

To fully reap the benefits of AI while maintaining the importance of human values and judgment in decision-making processes, human-AI collaboration is crucial.

10.2.1 Complementary Advantages:

- **The Analytical Capability of AI:** Artificial Intelligence is particularly good at digesting massive datasets, finding patterns, and accurately completing repeated jobs. This capacity allows for data-driven insights and increases efficiency.

- **Human Creativity and Judgment:** Humans provide creativity, ethical reasoning, and critical thinking. Making conclusions that are ethically sound and well-rounded requires combining AI's analytical capabilities with human judgment.

10.2.2 Strengthening Cooperation:

- **Interactive Interfaces:** Create approachable user interfaces that enable productive communication between people and AI systems. These user interfaces ought to make it simple for consumers to comprehend and manage AI operations.

- **Collaborative Decision-Making:** Establish frameworks for collaborative decision-making where humans make the final call based on their judgment and AI offers data-driven recommendations. This method makes use of both human and artificial intelligence strengths.

10.2.3 Training and Adaptation:

- **Skills Development:** Teach people how to work with AI systems in an efficient manner. Understanding AI's capabilities, interpreting its findings, and applying its insights to decision-making should be the main topics of training.

- **Adaptability**: Make sure AI systems can change to accommodate evolving human requirements and environments. User feedback is continuously used to develop AI systems and increase their efficacy in cooperative environments.

10.3 Ongoing Education and Development - Ensuring the Ethical Evolution of AI Systems

Over time, AI systems' efficacy and moral integrity depend heavily on ongoing learning and development.

10.3.1 Iterative Development:

- **Feedback Loops:** Create feedback loops to collect user feedback and assess AI system performance on a regular basis. Feedback keeps AI systems efficient and in line with user needs by pointing out areas for development.

- **Modifications and Enhancements:** Update and improve AI systems frequently in response to user feedback, fresh findings, and changing ethical norms. System performance is improved and new problems are addressed with the aid of continuous improvement.

10.3.2 Ethical Surveillance:

- **Ethical Examinations:** Conduct ethical audits on a regular basis to evaluate the effects of AI systems on society. Audits ought to assess things like impartiality, equity, and compliance with moral standards.

- **Accounts of Transparency:** Release open-access reports that provide information about the AI systems' development procedures, selection standards, and impact evaluations. Reports on transparency make it easier for stakeholders to comprehend how AI systems work and develop.

10.3.3 Encouraging Ethical Culture:

- **Organizational Commitment:** Encourage ethical AI development within your organization. This entails advancing moral standards, fostering moral judgment, and offering instruction on moral issues with artificial intelligence.

- **Partnership with Specialists:** Work together with researchers, industry professionals, and ethicists to stay up to date on ethical concerns and best practices. Interacting with specialists guarantees that AI systems develop in accordance with moral standards.

10.4 Every Stakeholder Has a Role to Play in the Effort to Promote Ethical AI

The ethical development and application of AI necessitates cooperation from all parties participating in the AI ecosystem.

10.4.1 Researchers' and Developers' Role:

- **Ethical Design:** Ethical issues need to be given top priority by academics and developers when creating and deploying AI systems. This entails resolving any potential prejudices, maintaining openness, and safeguarding user privacy.

- **Industrial Responsibility:** Adopt ethical innovation strategies that strike a balance between the growth of technology and its ethical ramifications. Think about the long-term effects and possible social impact of AI breakthroughs.

10.4.2 The Role of Regulators and Policymakers:

- **Establishing Guidelines:** Regulators and policymakers ought to set precise rules and specifications for the creation and application of morally sound AI. These rules ought to cover things like accountability, openness, and prejudice.

- **Enforcement and Oversight:** Put in place procedures to monitor AI systems and enforce moral norms. Ensuring compliance with regulations and addressing ethical infractions are facilitated by routine oversight.

10.4.3 The Public's Role:

- **Education and Advocacy**: In order to promote moral AI practices and hold stakeholders responsible, the public is essential. Inform people on the ramifications of artificial intelligence and take part in debates over moral principles.

- **Participation:** As knowledgeable users, interact with AI systems, offering suggestions and promoting moral behavior. The development and application of AI technologies are shaped in ways that reflect society values through public participation.

10.4.4 The Role of Industry Partnerships:

- **Collaborative Efforts:** Promote alliances to further ethical AI practices amongst academic institutions, industry leaders, and non-governmental groups. Working together can spur innovation and set norms for the sector.

- **Exchanging Knowledge:** To encourage the development of ethical AI, companies should exchange best practices and expertise. Sharing knowledge collaboratively aids in addressing shared issues and advancing moral principles.

In conclusion, utilizing technology for social good, encouraging human-AI cooperation, guaranteeing ongoing ethical development, and including all stakeholders in a joint endeavor are all essential to creating a better future with AI. By concentrating on these areas, we may respect moral standards, make a positive impact on society, and fully utilize AI's disruptive potential.

ABOUT THE AUTHOR

 Author and thought leader in the IT field Taylor Royce is well known. He has a two-decade career and is an expert at tech trend analysis and forecasting, which enables a wide audience to understand complicated concepts.

Royce's considerable involvement in the IT industry stemmed from his passion with technology, which he developed during his computer science studies. He has extensive knowledge of the industry because of his experience in both software development and strategic consulting.

Known for his research and lucidity, he has written multiple best-selling books and contributed to esteemed tech periodicals. Translations of Royce's books throughout the world demonstrate his impact.

Royce is a well-known authority on emerging technologies and their effects on society, frequently requested as a speaker at international conferences and as a guest on tech podcasts. He promotes the development of ethical technology, emphasizing problems like data privacy and the digital divide.

In addition, with a focus on sustainable industry growth, Royce mentors upcoming tech experts and supports IT education projects. Taylor Royce is well known for his ability to combine analytical thinking with technical know-how. He sees a time when technology will ethically benefit humanity.

www.ingramcontent.com/pod-product-compliance
Lightning Source LLC
LaVergne TN
LVHW022125060326
832903LV00063B/4070